W 8/14

DEC 2011

LAUGH OUT LOUD!

THE SCHOOL'S COOL
JOKE BOOK

Sean Connolly and Kay Barnham

WINDMILL
BOOKS

New York

Published in 2012 by Windmill Books, LLC
303 Park Avenue South, Suite # 1280, New York, NY 10010-3657

First Edition

Editor: Joe Harris
Illustrations: Adam Clay and Dynamo Design
Layout Design: Notion Design

Library of Congress Cataloging-in-Publication Data

Connolly, Sean, 1956–
 The school's cool joke book / by Sean Connolly and Kay Barnham. — 1st ed.
    p. cm. — (Laugh out loud!)
 Includes index.
 ISBN 978-1-61533-363-9 (library binding) — ISBN 978-1-61533-401-8 (pbk.) — ISBN 978-1-61533-480-3
(6-pack)
 1. Schools—Juvenile humor. I. Barnham, Kay. II. Title.
 PN6231.S3C66 2012
 818'.602—dc22
                                          2010052142

Printed in China

For more great fiction and nonfiction, go to www.windmillbooks.com

CPSIA Compliance Information: Batch #AS2011WM: For Further Information contact Windmill Books, New York, New York at 1-866-478-0556
SL001837US

CONTENTS

SCHOOL'S COOL

What was the dentist's favorite subject at school?
Flossophy.

What did the number 0 say to the number 8?
"That's a cool belt."

What do you get if you cross a vampire and a teacher?
Blood tests.

Why did the
teacher wear
sunglasses?
Because his class
was so bright.

Why did the
teacher jump into
the swimming
pool?
He wanted to test
the water.

What kind of lunches do geometry teachers enjoy?
Square meals.

Principal: You'll start with a salary of $25,000 and then go up to $35,000 in six months.
Teacher: In that case I think I would like to start in six months!

Why was the cross-eyed teacher's class rioting?
She couldn't control her pupils.

Why was the broom late for school?
It overswept.

Teacher: Who invented King Arthur's round table?
Pupil: Was it Sir Cumference?

Did you hear about the cannibal that was expelled from school?
He was buttering up the teachers.

Teacher: What language do they speak in Cuba?
Pupil: Cubic!

Why did one pencil tell the other pencil that it looked old and tired?
Because it was blunt.

What's the tastiest class at school?
History. It's full of dates.

My music teacher said I have a heavenly voice!
That's not strictly true—she said your voice was like
nothing on Earth!

Teacher: You missed school yesterday, didn't you?
Pupil: Not very much!

Why did the pupil think the teacher had a crush on him?
She put "X"s all over his
homework.

Teacher: Why are you taking that
sponge into class?
Pupil: Because I find your classes
so absorbing!

What is a polygon?
A dead parrot.

Why was the math textbook
miserable?
It had too many problems.

Why was the music teacher locked out of his classroom?
The keys were on the piano.

English teacher: Give me an example of a long sentence.
Pupil: Life imprisonment.

What did the pencil say to the protractor?
Take me to your ruler.

I sprained my ankle and had to miss gym for 2 weeks.
Lucky you. Our gym teacher never accepts a lame excuse for his class!

Why don't leopards bother to cheat in exams?
Because they know that they will always be spotted!

SCHOOL'S COOL

Is the math teacher in
a good mood today?
I wouldn't count on it!

Teacher: Can you
define the word
"hardship"?
Silly pupil: Is it a
boat made out of
concrete?

My math teacher is
a real peach!
You mean she's pretty?
No—I mean she has a heart of stone!

What do history teachers do before they get married?
They go out on dates!

Why is 6 afraid of 7?
Because 7 ate 9!

Parent: Why have you given my son such a bad grade in his report card? He's as intelligent as the next boy!

Teacher: Yes, but the next boy is an idiot!

Teacher: Eat up your school lunch—it's full of iron.

Pupil: That explains why it's so difficult to chew!

Teacher: How did people spend their time in the Stone Age?

Pupil: Did they listen to rock music?

Parent: Do you think my son has what it takes to be a pilot?

Teacher: Well, he certainly spends plenty of time with his head in the clouds!

What happens when music teachers are sick?
They send in a note!

Why was the archaeology teacher unhappy?
Her career was in ruins.

History teacher: How would
you discover what life in
Ancient Egypt was really
like?
Pupil: I'd ask my mummy!

Did you hear about the math
teacher whose mistakes
started to multiply?
In the end, they had to take
him away!

Why does your teacher have
her hair in a bun?
Because she has a face like
a burger!

Teacher: What is the plural of baby?
Pupil: Twins!

Why do kindergarten teachers have such a positive attitude?
They know how to make the little things count.

Parent: Do you think my son will make a good Arctic explorer?
Teacher: I would think so: most of his grades are below zero!

Teacher: Can you tell me what water is?
Pupil: It's a colorless liquid that turns black when I put my hands in it!

Why is that boy locked up in a cage in the corner of the classroom?
Oh, he's the teacher's pet!

I think our school must be haunted.
Why?
Because the principal keeps talking about the school spirit!

Teacher: Who discovered Pluto?
Pupil: Walt Disney!

Teacher: What do Attila the Hun and Winnie the Pooh have in common?
Pupil: They have the same middle name!

Teacher: Michael, how do we know that the Earth is round?
Michael: I didn't say it was, Mr. Johnson!

Teacher: If you multiply 245 by 3,456 and divide the answer by 165, then subtract 752, what will you get?
Pupil: The wrong answer!

Teacher: How good are you at picking up music?
Pupil: Well, I'm not sure if I could lift a whole piano!

Teacher: Mary, how did you find the questions in your English test?
Mary: Oh, I found the questions easily enough—it's the answers I couldn't find!

Teacher: Please don't talk while you are doing your exam.
Pupil: It's all right, Miss Brown. We're not doing the exam—just talking!

Teacher: Who invented fractions?
Pupil: Henry the Eighth!

Where do vampire schoolchildren go for field trips?
Lake Eerie!

SCHOOL'S COOL

How does a math teacher remove hard wax from his ears?
He works it out with a pencil!

Teacher: Why were you late this morning, Veronica?
Veronica: I squeezed the toothpaste too hard, and it took me half an hour to get it all back into the tube again!

Pupil: Can we do some work on the Iron Age today?
Teacher: Well, I'm not certain, I'm a bit rusty on that period of history!

Ten cats were at the movies. One walked out. How many were left?
None—they were all copycats!

Teacher: What's a computer byte?
Pupil: I didn't even know they had teeth!

SCHOOL'S COOL

What happened after the wheel was first invented?
It caused a revolution!

Teacher: Did you know that most accidents happen in the kitchen?
Pupil: Yes, but we still have to eat them!

Mom: Time to get up and go to school!
Son: I don't want to go! Everyone hates me and I get bullied!
Mom: But you have to go— you're the principal!

Teacher: How many seconds are there in a year?
Pupil: Twelve—January 2nd, February 2nd...

What did the music teacher need a ladder for?
Reaching the high notes!

SCHOOL'S COOL

I banged my head on the locker door this morning!
Have you seen the school nurse?
No, just stars!

Teacher: Why is your homework late, young man?
Pupil: Sorry, Miss Elliot, my dad is a slow writer!

How do archaeologists get into locked tombs, young man?
Do they use a skeleton key, Mr. Edwards?

Math teacher: What are net profits?
Pupil: What fishermen have left after paying the crew!

I'm not really interested in math: I just go along to the lesson to make up the numbers!

What was the blackbird doing in the school library?
Looking for bookworms!

Did you hear about the gym teacher who used to run around the classroom in order to jog pupils' memories?

Why did the school orchestra have such awful manners?
Because it didn't know how to conduct itself!

Teacher: In the future, all trains and buses will run on time.
Pupil: Won't they run on fuel, just like now?

SCHOOL'S COOL

Teacher: I wish you'd pay a little attention!
Pupil: I'm paying as little as I can!

Teacher: How did people react when electricity was first discovered?
Pupil: They got a nasty shock!

Young man, I hope I don't catch you cheating in the math test!
So do I, Miss Goldman!

What is a science teacher's favorite breed of dog?
A Lab!

When do 2 and 2 make more than 4?
When they make 22!

Sign outside the music department:
Violin for sale. Good price—no strings attached!

Teacher: Why was the invention of the safety match an important change?
Pupil: It was a striking achievement!

Why did the school cafeteria hire a dentist?
To make more filling meals!

Parent: Do you think my son could work as a DJ on the radio?
Teacher: He certainly has the face for it!

Why are teachers always welcome in pool halls?
Because they always bring their own chalk!

How do you know your school bus is old?
The seats are covered in mammoth hide!

Why did the burglar
break into the music
department?
He was after the lute!

Why was Cinderella
terrible at sports?
Because her coach
was a pumpkin!

Did you hear about the
math teacher and the
art teacher who used to go out together?
They spent their time painting by numbers!

Teacher: This homework looks as though it has been
written by your father.
Pupil: Of course it does—I borrowed his pen!

Teacher: Which two words in the English language have
the most letters?
Pupil: "Post Office!"

Teacher: Where were all the kings and queens of France crowned?
Pupil: On the head!

Teacher: Which age did the mummies live in?
Pupil: The Band-Age!

Where did King Arthur's men get their training?
At knight school!

What were the 16 schoolboys playing in the telephone booth?
Squash!

What sort of ring is always square?
A boxing ring!

SCHOOL'S COOL

How many librarians does it take to change a lightbulb?
Two. One to screw it in and one to say, "Shhhhhhh!" at the squeaking noise.

Book seen in the school library:
The Survivors' Guide to Escaping from a Sinking Ship by Mandy Lifeboats

What do you say to the school's best pole vaulter?
Hiya!

What goes putt-putt-putt-putt-putt?
The worst golfer on the school team.

Why did the silly schoolkid buy a seahorse?
Because he wanted to play water polo!

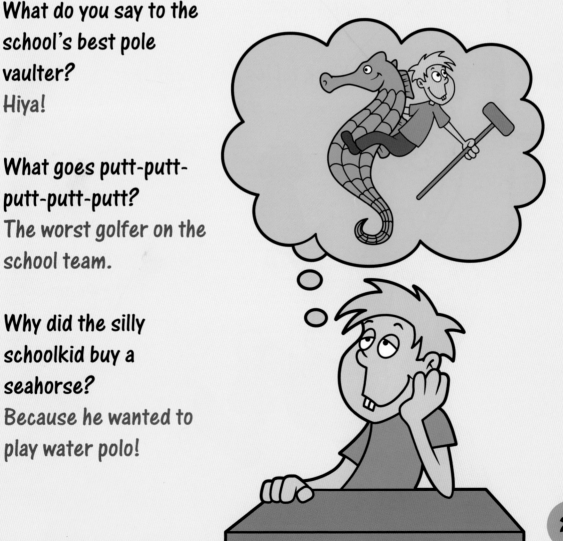

Mom: Why didn't you come straight home from school?
Daughter: Because we live around the corner!

Where do you find a giant scholar?
Around the neck of a giant's shirt.

In a family with seven children, why was the youngest late for school?
The alarm was set for six.

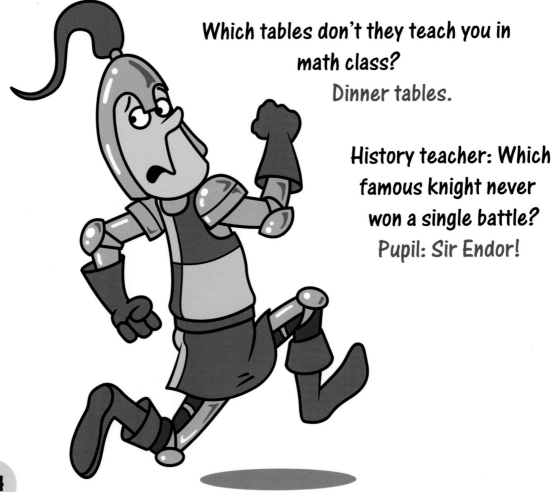

Which tables don't they teach you in math class?
Dinner tables.

History teacher: Which famous knight never won a single battle?
Pupil: Sir Endor!

Teacher: What was Robin Hood's mom called?
Pupil: Mother Hood.

Teacher: What is the plural of mouse?
Pupil: Mice!
Teacher: And what is the plural of house?
Pupil: Hice!

What's the difference between a train and a teacher?
A train says "choo choo" but a teacher says, "Take that gum out of your mouth this instant!"

What did the IT teacher name his baby son?
Chip.

Teacher: What is a myth?
Pupil: A female moth!

SCHOOL'S COOL

Teacher: Our school cafeteria is spotlessly clean.
Pupil: Is that why the food always tastes of soap?

Teacher: How do you make a sick insect better?
Pupil: Give it a "T," then it will be a stick insect!

Geography teacher: Young man, where is Turkey?
Pupil: No idea, sir, I haven't seen it since
Thanksgiving!

Music teacher: What sort of music can you make with
your feet?
Pupil: Sole music!

SCHOOL'S COOL

Why did the school cook become a history teacher?
She was an expert on ancient grease!

What happens to old French teachers?
One day they realize that un oeuf is enough!

Well, son, how did you find your geography test?
With a map and compass—how else!

Teacher: Young man, I think you need glasses.
Pupil: What makes you think that, Mr. Adams?
Teacher: You're facing the wrong way!

Today is flying saucer day at the school cafeteria.
How come?
Because we get unidentified frying objects!

Teacher: If I gave you $10 a week for the next six months what would you have?
Pupil: A crazy teacher!

English teacher: For tonight's homework I want you to write an essay on Moby Dick.
Pupil: I can't do that, Miss Schneider!
Teacher: Why on earth not?
Pupil: I don't have any waterproof ink!

Why did the Cyclops have to retire from teaching?
He only had one pupil!

What is a math teacher's favorite dessert?
Apple pi.

Music teacher: What do you get if you drop a piano down a mineshaft?
Pupil: A flat minor!

Teacher: Which part of a fish weighs the most?
Pupil: The scales!

Science teacher: Why do doctors and nurses wear masks in the hospital operating room?
Pupil: So if they make a mistake, no one will know who did it!

Teacher: Did your mom or dad help you with these questions?
Pupil: No, I got them wrong all by myself!

Science teacher: Fred, what food do giraffes eat?
Pupil: Neck-tarines!

Teacher: Why were you late for school today?
Pupil: I got a flat tire on my bicycle.
Teacher: Did you run over some broken glass?
Pupil: No, there was a fork in the road!

NO MORE DANDRUFF

History teacher: Why was the guillotine invented?
Pupil: As a cure for dandruff?

Why did the flea get expelled from flea school?
He just wasn't up to scratch!

Teacher: In this exam you will be allowed 15 minutes for each question.
Pupil: How long do we get for the answers?

Science teacher: Harry, how would you fix a short circuit?
Pupil: Add some more wire to make it longer, Mr. Johnson?

Geography teacher: Annette, what can you tell me about the Dead Sea?
Pupil: I didn't even know it was sick!

SCHOOL'S COOL

Teacher: Where is the easiest place to find diamonds?
Pupil: In a deck of cards!

I've always had a hard time with decimals—I just can't see the point!

Pupil: I don't think I deserved a zero in this test.
Teacher: I agree—but it's the lowest mark I could give you!

What do you call the worst player on the school football team?
The drawback!

How did the school orchestra leader survive being hit by lightning?
They had a very bad conductor!

Glossary

archaeology (AR-kee-OH-loh-jee) the study of ancient remains

byte (BITE) a measurement of information on a computer

geometry (jee-OH-muh-tree) an area of math concerned with shapes

guillotine (GILL-oh-teen) a machine for cutting off heads that was used in the French Revolution

mineshaft (MINE-shaft) a long tunnel that leads into a mine

protractor (pro-TRAK-tur) a tool for measuring angles

Further Reading

Trimmer, Tony. *Seriously Silly School Jokes.* New York: Kingfisher, 2005.

Winter, Judy A. *Jokes About School.* Mankato, MN: Capstone Press, 2010.

Yoe, Craig. *The Mighty Big Book of School Jokes.* New York: Price Stern Sloan, 2003.

Index

Web Sites

For Web resources related to the subject of this book, go to: www.windmillbooks.com/weblinks and select this book's title.